ABCs for Kids
Cross Stitch Alphabets

From whimsical and quirky to sweet and traditional this book is filled with delightful alphabets for the children in your life.

Well-known cross stitch designers Linda Gillum, Sandy Orton, and Donna Yuen share eight alphabet samplers for kids—newborns to tweens—to add a special touch of color and fun to their room décor. The Noah's Ark alphabet is perfect for the newborn and little girls are sure to love In the Garden with its sweet rosebuds and butterflies. Boys, on the other hand, will find the Alphabots enticing—robot letters made with all sorts of mechanical parts. The Bugs All Around and Fiesta Folk Art alphabets with their vibrant colors will bring smiles at any age and the Once Upon a Time fairy tale and script alphabets are classic favorites. What a fun way to learn the ABCs!

Included with the alphabet letters is a wonderful array of small motifs that can be used in combination with individual letters to create door signs, wall hangings, and labels, or embellishments for clothing and quilts. Use the alphabets to personalize to your heart's content. With just a little imagination the possibilities are endless and, without doubt, your hand stitched creations are sure to be cherished.

Alphabots by Sandy Orton p.18

ABC Thingumajigs by Linda Gillum p.30

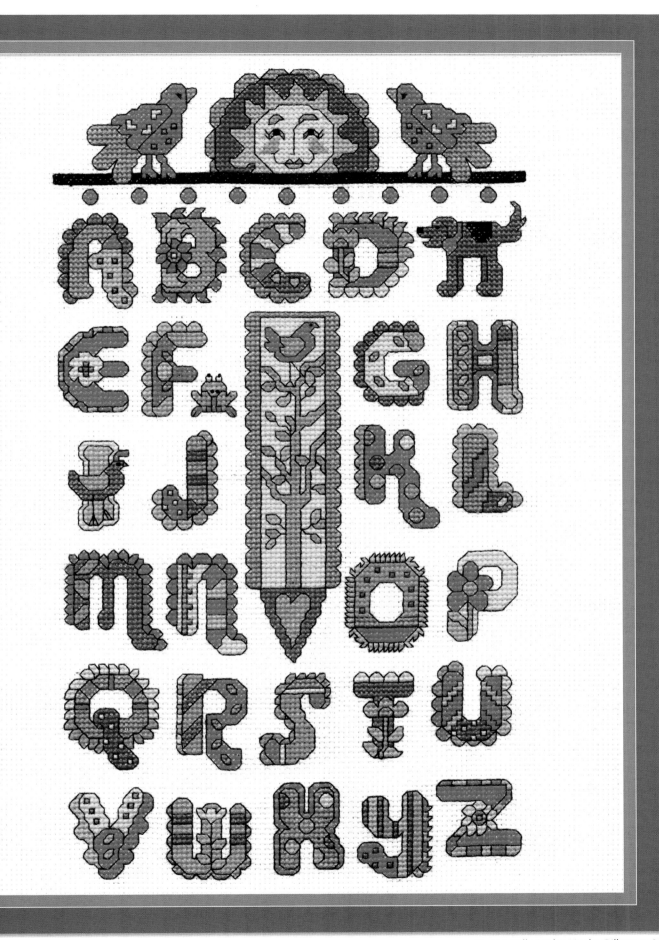

Fiesta Folk Art by Linda Gillum p.32

In the Garden by Sandy Orton p.11

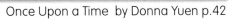
Once Upon a Time by Donna Yuen p.42

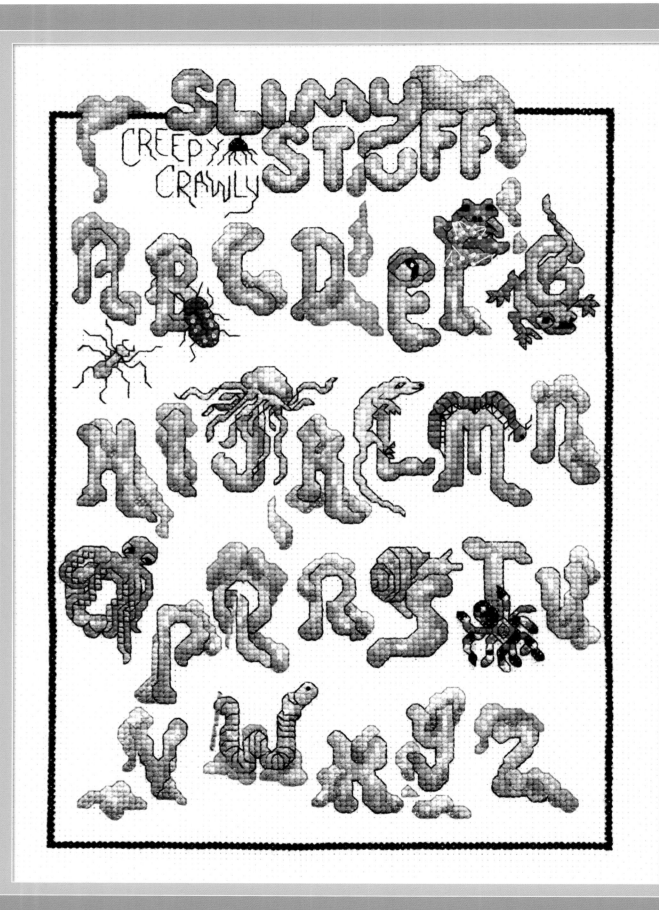

Creepy Crawly by Linda Gillum p.38

Bugs All Around by Linda Gillum p.36

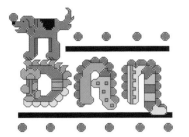

Here are just a few examples of the endless ways to use the eight alphabets in this book. Choose letters from a single alphabet or mix and match for the perfect combination. Personalize a child's room with a special door sign or make clever labels for organizing belongings. It's best to use color copies of the alphabets to layout your designs on paper before you start stitching. Photocopy the grid on the back inside cover for help in charting your designs. No rules here, just use your imagination and your creations are sure to please both the young and the young at heart.

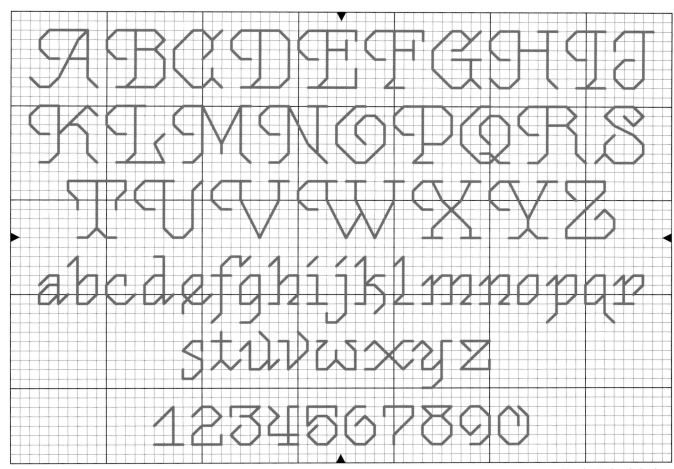

Backstitch Alphabet

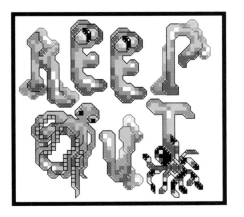

In the Garden
Backstitch Alphabet

DMC	BS
844	✎

11

In the Garden
Size: 181 x 129

DMC	X	1/4	BS	Str	FK
1	◈	◈			•
164	◣	◣			
340	✕	✕			
341	H	H			
603	♥	♥		✎	
604	⊥	⊥	•	✎	
605	Z	Z			
645				✎	• •
772	I	I	•	✎	
844	■	■	•	✎	° •
844				✎	•

Key continued on next page

Key continued

DMC	X	1/4
912	↑	↑
954	m	m
955	2	
958	◆	◆
964	⊁	⊁
3747	‡	‡
3823	⊠	⊠
3855	★	★

•2-ply
°3-ply

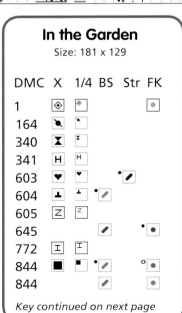

In the Garden

Size: 181 x 129

DMC	X	1/4	BS	Str	FK
1	◈	◈			●
164	◣	◣			
340	✕	✕			
341	H	H			
603	♥	♥		╱	
604	⊥	⊥	●	╱	
605	Z	Z		╱	
645				╱	● ●
772	I	I			
844	■	■	●	╱	○ ●
844				╱	●

Key continued on next page

Key continued

DMC	X	1/4
912	↑	↑
954	m	m
955	2	
958	◆	◆
964	⋊	⋊
3747	‡	‡
3823	⋈	⋈
3855	★	★

•2-ply
°3-ply

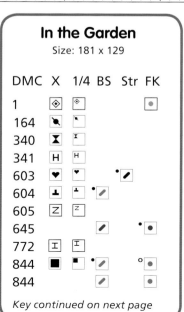

In the Garden
Size: 181 x 129

DMC	X	1/4	BS	Str	FK
1	⬖	⬖			•
164	◣	◢			
340	✕	✕			
341	H	H			
603	♥	♥		╱	
604	⊥	⊥	•	╱	
605	z	z			
645				╱	•
772	I	I			
844	■	■	•	╱	•
844				╱	•

Key continued on next page

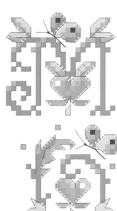

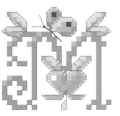

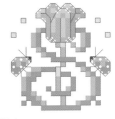

Garden

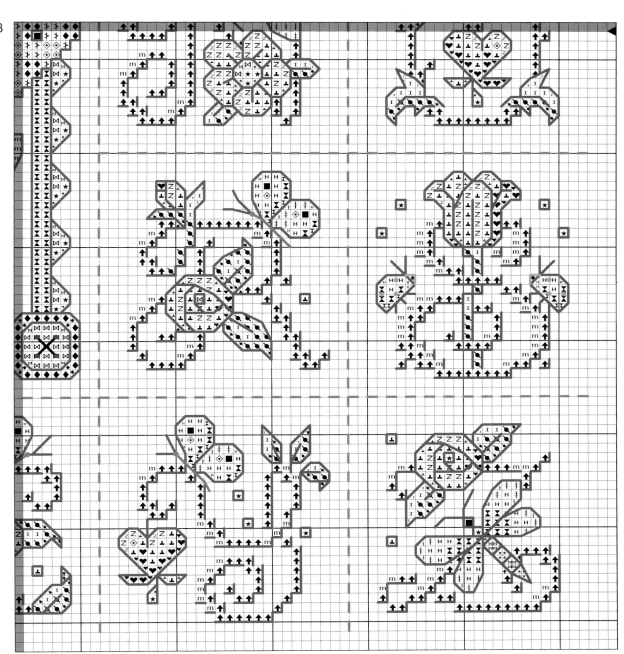

Key continued

DMC	X	1/4
912	↑	↑
954	m	m
955	2	
958	◆	◆
964	⟩	⟩
3747	‡	‡
3823	⋈	⋈
3855	★	★

•2-ply
°3-ply

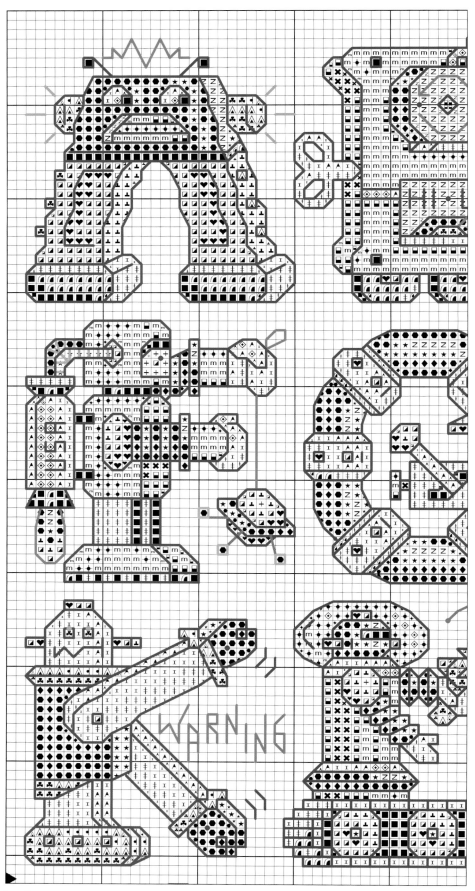

Alphabots
Size: 141 x 181

DMC	X	1/4	BS	FK
1	◈	◈		⊙
157	✦	✦		
349	♥	♥	•⟋	•⊙
350	◪	◪		
352	⊥	⊥		
353	+	+		
413	◰	◰		
415	I	I		
472	◂|	◂|		
702	♣	♣	•⟋	
704	△	△		
725	●	●		
744	★	★		
762	▲	▲		
783	◆	◆	⟋	
797	✕	✕		
798	■	■	•⟋	•⊙
799	m	m		
3078	Z	Z		
3371	■	■	⟋	•⊙
3371			•⟋	
*414	‡	‡		
*318				

*Use one strand of each
•2-ply

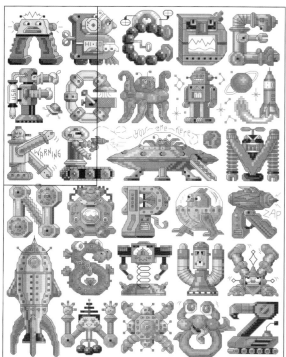

Top 1

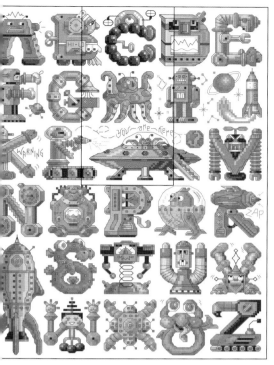

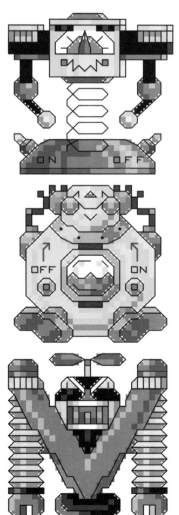

June 2, 2006

Top 3

Alphabots

Size: 141 x 181

DMC	X	1/4	BS	FK
1	◈	◈		●
157	✦	✦		
349	♥	♥	•/	•●
350	◪	◪		
352	┴	┴		
353	+	+		
413	◜	◜		
415	Ι	Ι		
472	◀	◀		
702	♣	♣	•/	
704	Δ	Δ		
725	⬢	⬢		
744	★	★		
762	⋀	⋀		
783	◆	◆	/	
797	✖	✖		
798	⬓	⬓	•/	•●
799	m	m		
3078	Z	Z		
3371	■	■	/	•●
3371			•/	
*414 / *318	‡	‡		

*Use one strand of each
•2-ply

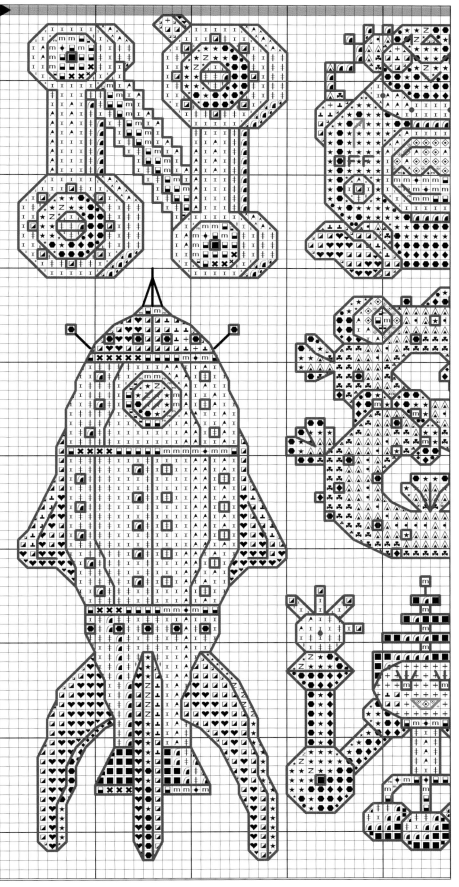

Bottom 1

21

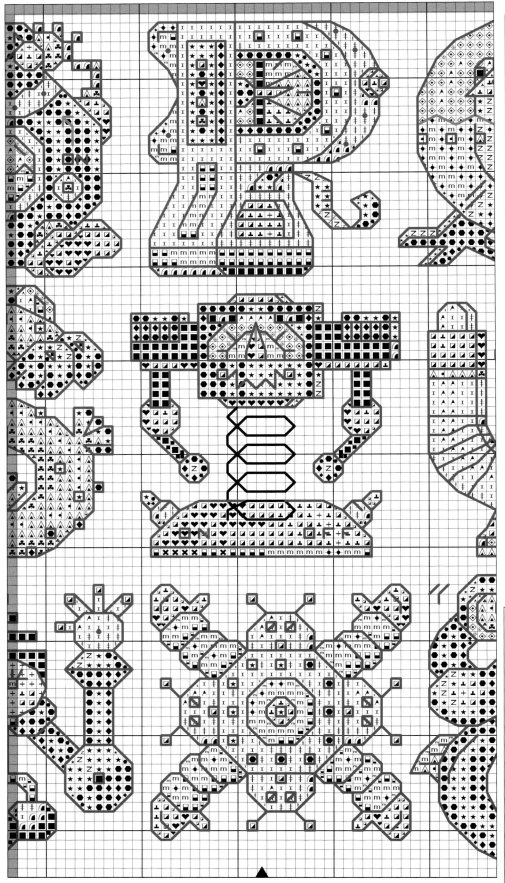

Bottom 2

DMC	X	1/4	BS	FK
1	◈	◇		•
157	✦	⁺		
349	♥	♥	•╱	•⊡
350	◪	◪		
352	⊥	⊥		
353	⁺	⁺		
413	◤	◤		
415	I	I		
472	◀	◀		
702	♣	♣	•╱	
704	◭	◭		
725	●	●		
744	★	★		
762	◮	◮		
783	◆	◆	╱	
797	✖	✖		
798	⊟	⊟	•╱	•⊡
799	m	m		
3078	Z	z		
3371	■	■	╱	•●
3371			•╱	
*414 }	‡	‡		
*318 }				

*Use one strand of each
•2-ply

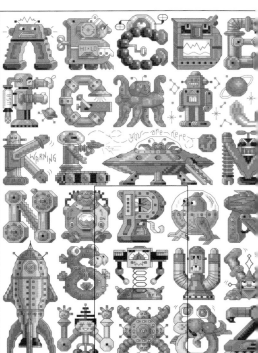

22

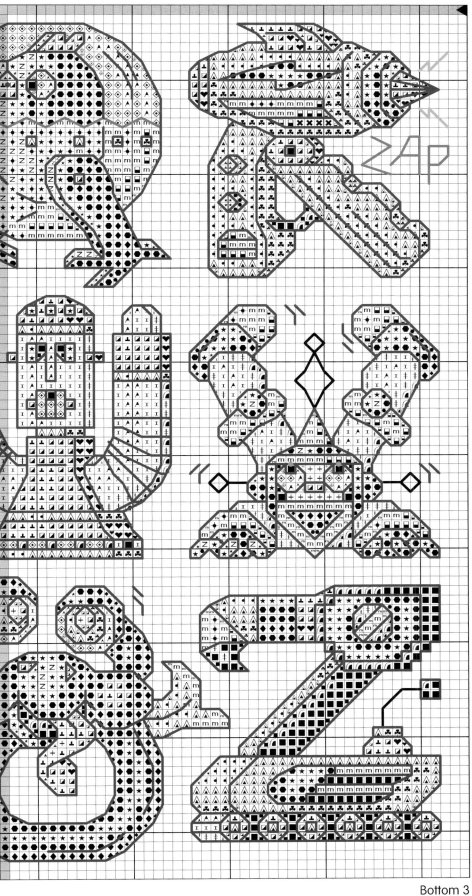

Bottom 3

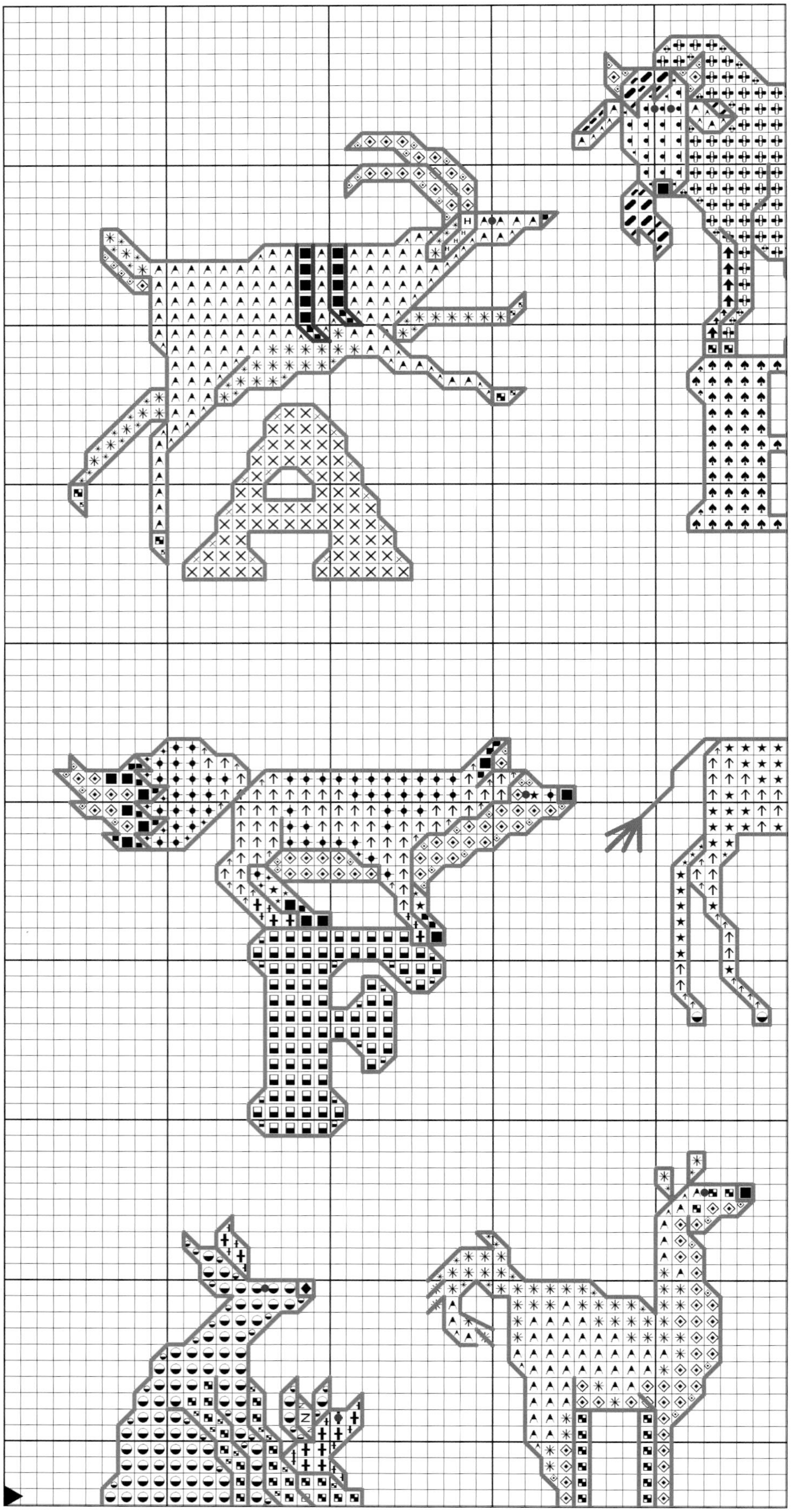

Top 1

Noah's Ark

Size: 140 x 183

DMC	X	1/4	BS	FK
1	◈	◈		
210	⋈	⋈		
310	■	■	/	•
318	◒	◒		
322	♣	♣	/	
340	∩	∩		
351	●	●		
352	×	×		
353	Z	Z		
414	✝	✝		
433	/	/	/	
436	✳	✳		
603	♥	♥		•
605	H	H		
738	▲	▲		

Key continued on next page

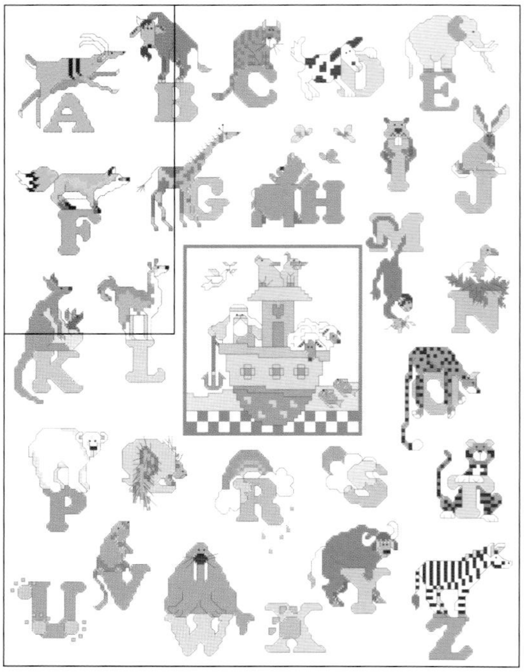

Key continued

DMC	X	1/4	BS	FK
744	⊥	⊥		
762	◨	◪		
772	◮	◭		
775	L	L		
840	↑	↑		
841	⊷	⊶		
842	◀	◁		
954	♠	♠		
955	U	U		
3325	⊠	⊠		
3608	✿	○		
3776	★	★		
3799	◆	◆	/	•
3846	◧	◧		
3854	✦	+		
3856	↑	↑		

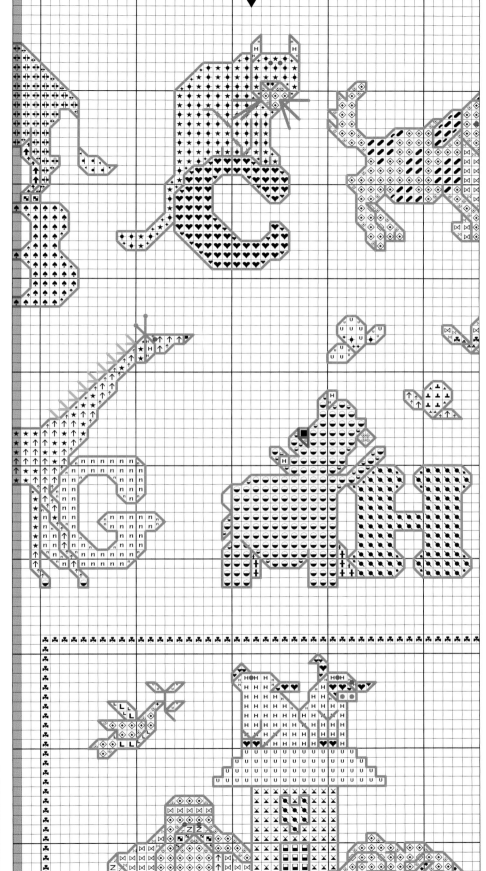

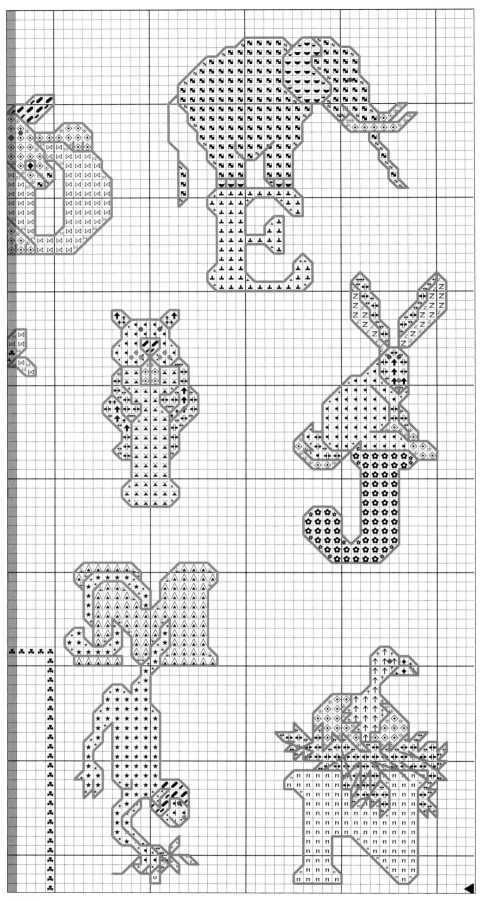

DMC	X	1/4	BS	FK
1	◈	◈		
210	⋈	⋈		
310	■	■	／	●
318	◗	◖		
322	♣	✳	／	
340	ⁿ	ⁿ		
351	◣	◣		
352	✕	✕		
353	Z	Z		
414	✚	✚		
433	◢	◢	／	
436	✳	✳		
603	♥	♥		●
605	H	H		
738	▲	▲		

Key continued on next page

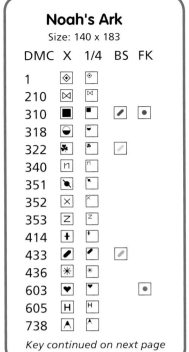

Top 3

26

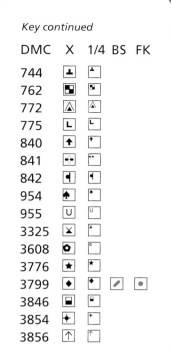

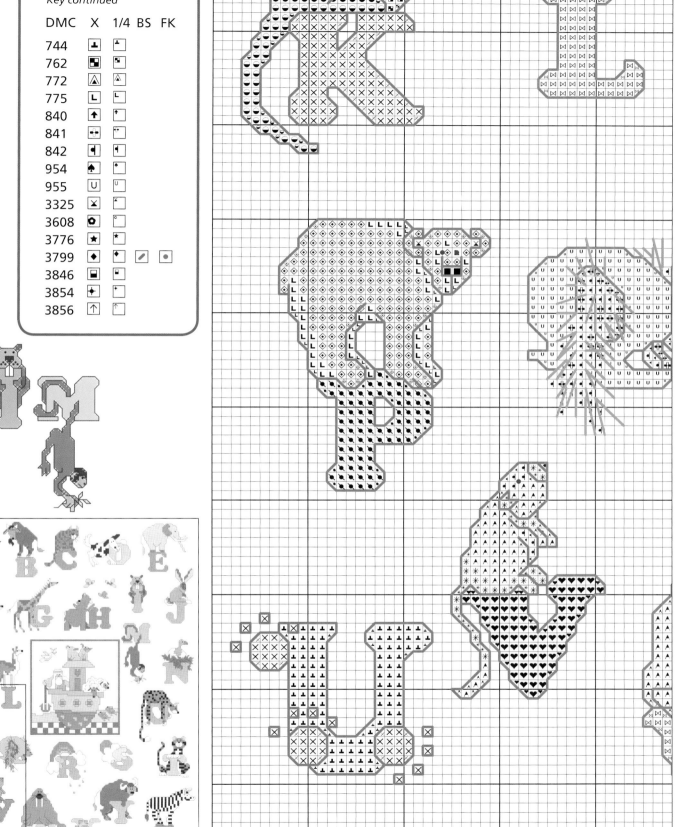

Bottom 1

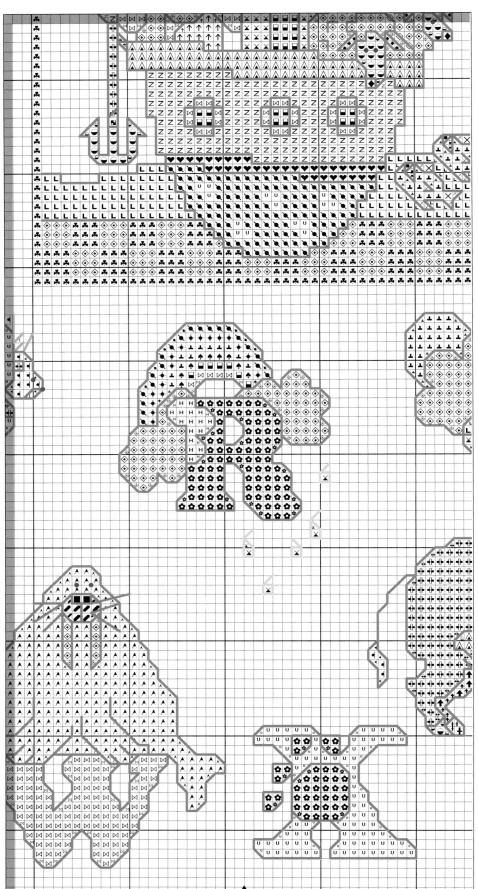

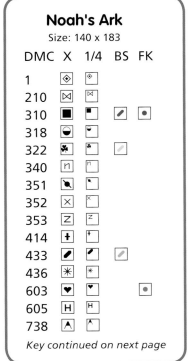

Noah's Ark

Size: 140 x 183

DMC	X	1/4	BS	FK
1	◈	◈		
210	⋈	⋈		
310	■	■	✎	●
318	◗	◗		
322	♣	♣	✎	
340	n	n		
351	◥	◥		
352	✕	✕		
353	Z	z		
414	✚	✚		
433	◢	◢	✎	
436	✳	✳		
603	♥	♥		●
605	H	H		
738	▲	▲		

Key continued on next page

Bottom 2

Key continued

DMC	X	1/4	BS	FK
744	⊥	⊥		
762	▣	▣		
772	◭	◭		
775	L	L		
840	↑	↑		
841	⊶	⊶		
842	◀	◀		
954	♠	♠		
955	U	U		
3325	✕	✕		
3608	●	°		
3776	★	★		
3799	◆	◆	╱	●
3846	▣	▣		
3854	✦	✦		
3856	↑	↑		

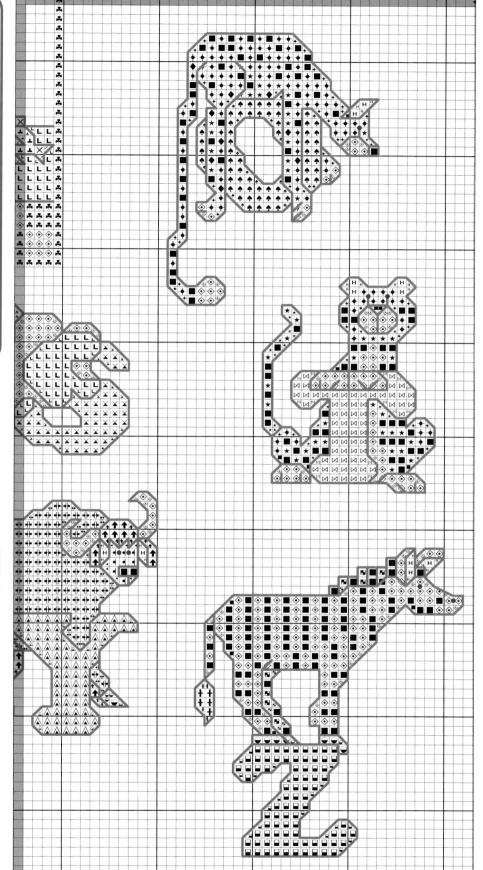

Bottom 3

29

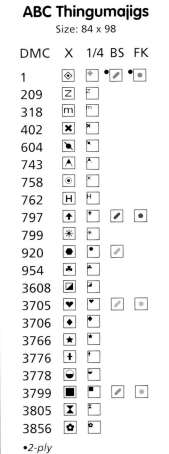

ABC Thingumajigs

Size: 84 x 98

DMC	X	1/4	BS	FK
1	◈	◈	•/	••
209	Z	Z		
318	m	m		
402	✖	✗		
604	◣	◣		
743	▲	▲		
758	⊙	⊙		
762	H	H		
797	↑	↑	/	•
799	✳	✳		
920	●	●	/	
954	♣	♣		
3608	◪	◪		
3705	♥	♥	/	•
3706	◆	◆		
3766	★	★		
3776	✚	✚		
3778	◓	◓	/	
3799	■	■	/	•
3805	✖	✖		
3856	✿	✿		

•2-ply

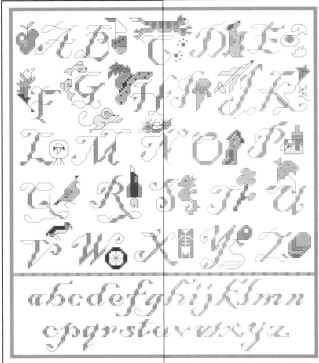

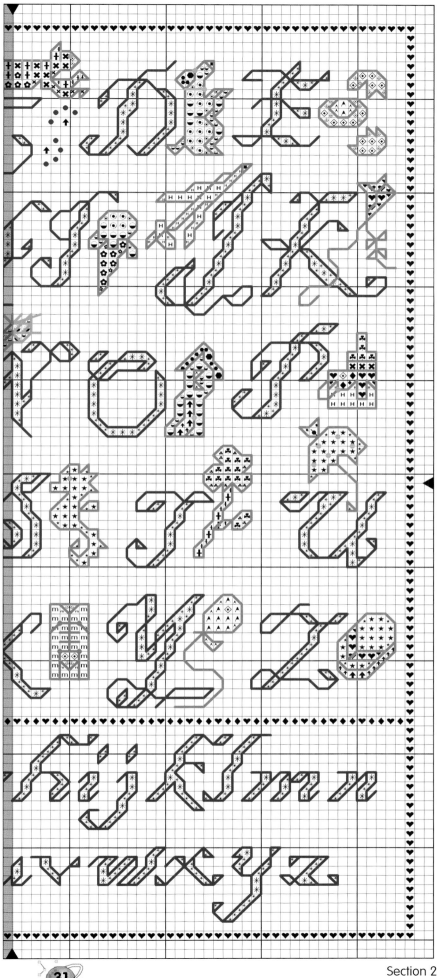

Section 2

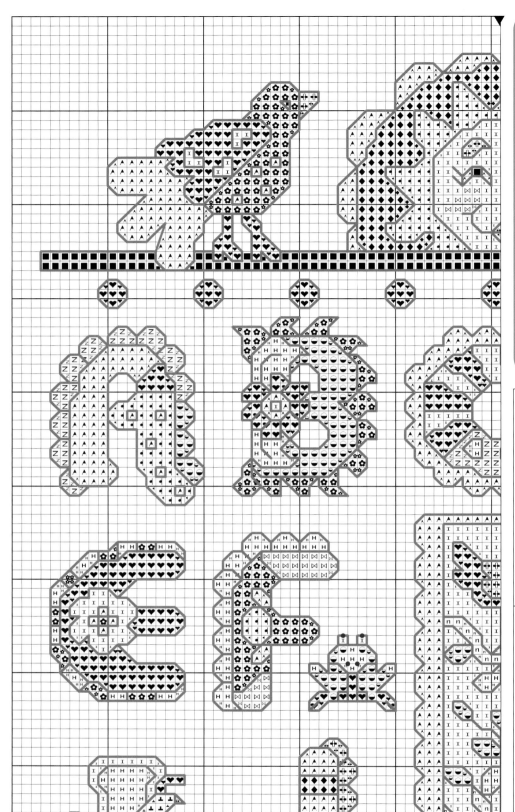

Fiesta Folk Art

Size: 98 x 168

DMC	X	1/4	BS	FK
208	ꝣ	ꝣ		
310	■	◼	╱	●
603	⧖	⧖		
606	♥	♥		
722	◀	◀		
743	I	I		
798	◆	◆		
906	◓	◓		
907	H	H		
971	✛	✛		
976	ᴎ	ᴎ		
3607	✿	✿		
3746	⊥	⊥		
3845	▲	▲		

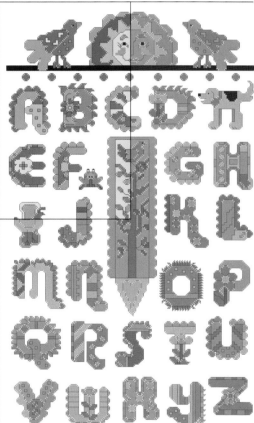

Top 1

32

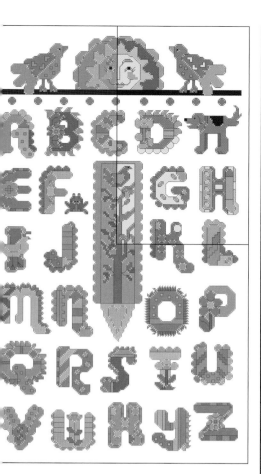

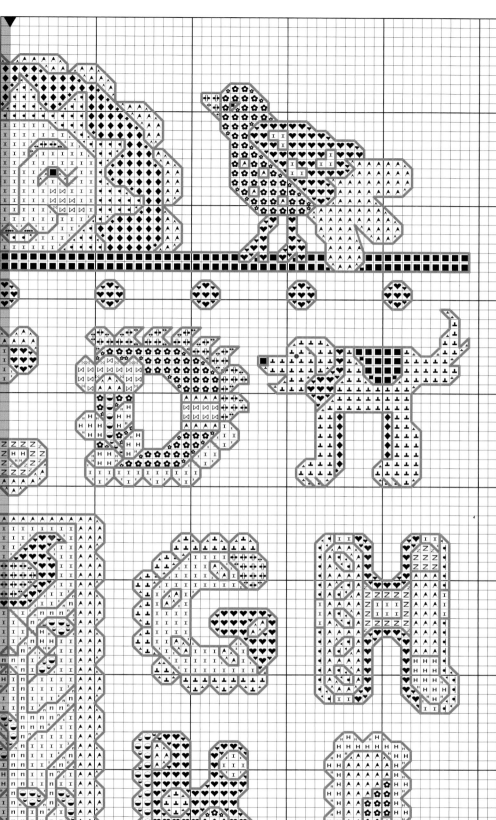

Top 2

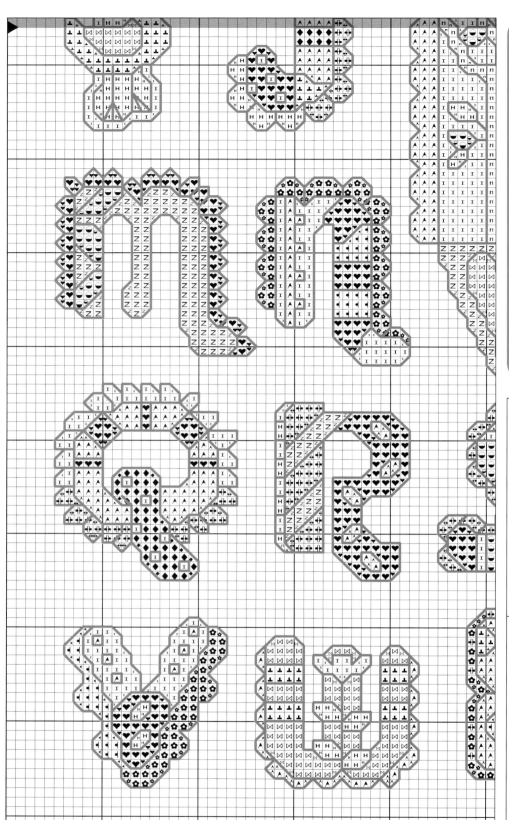

Fiesta Folk Art
Size: 98 x 168

DMC	X	1/4	BS	FK
208	Z	Z		
310	■	■	/	●
603	⋈	⋈		
606	♥	♥		
722	◢	◢		
743	I	I		
798	◆	◆		
906	◓	◓		
907	H	H		
971	⟷	⟷		
976	n	n		
3607	✿	✿		
3746	⊥	⊥		
3845	A	A		

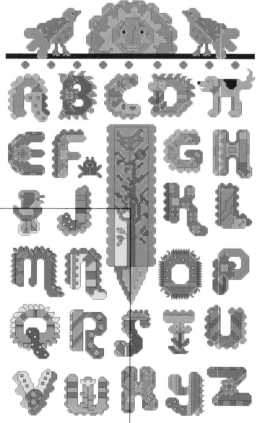

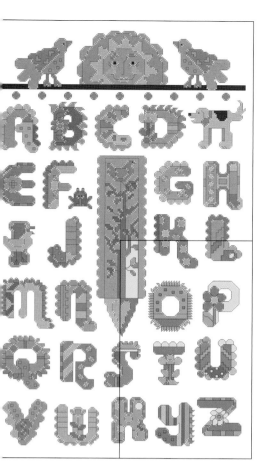

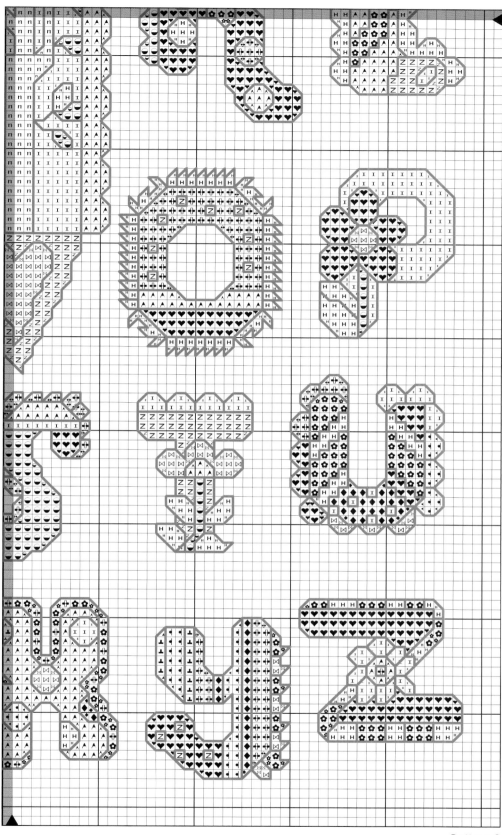

Bottom 2

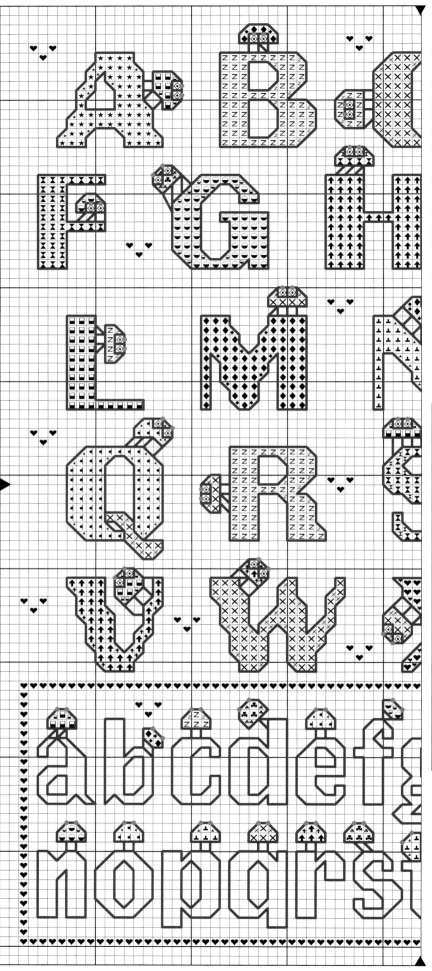

Bugs All Around

Size: 84 x 98

DMC	X	1/4	BS	FK
1	◇			
155	★	★		
208	⊠	⊡		
310			▨	●
606	▣	▪		
666	♥	♥		
740	⊥	⊥		
741	◒	◓		
743	Z	z		
906	♣	♣		
907	✕	✗		
3608	◆	◆		
3805	↑	↑		
3846	◪	◪		

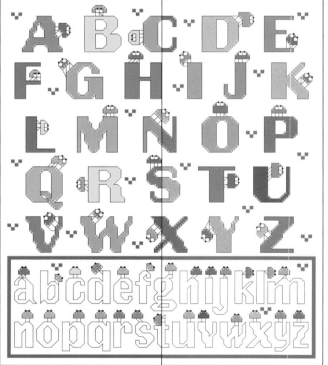

Section 1

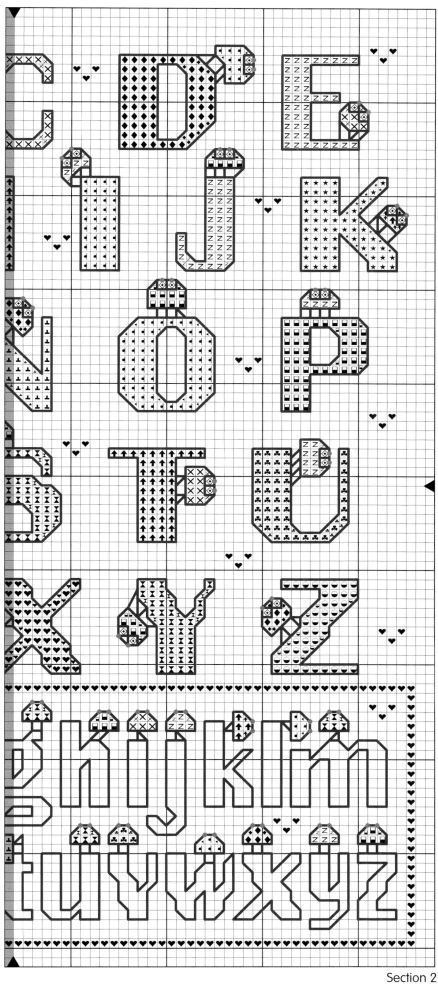

ABCDE
FGHIJK
LMNOP
QRSTU
VWXYZ

abcdefghijklm
nopqrstuvwxyz

Zack's
Room

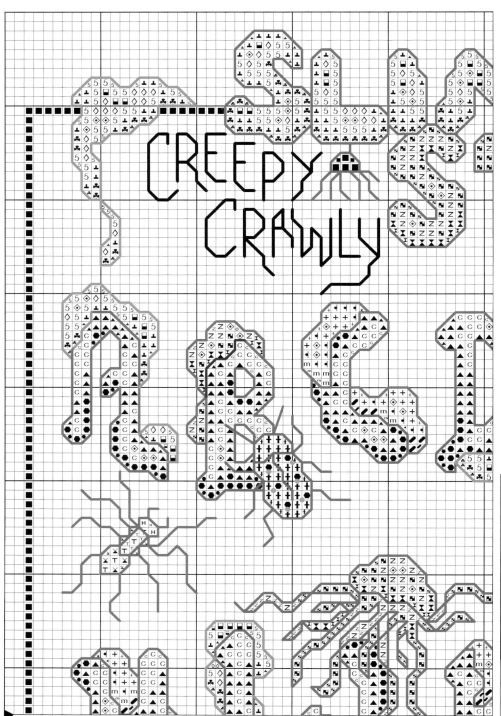

Top 1

Creepy Crawly
Size: 99 x 146

DMC	X	1/4	BS	FK
1	◈	◐	•⟋	⊙
165	▣	▣		
208	▰	▰	⟋	
209	m	m		
210	◀	◀		
211	+	+		
304	◆	◆		
310	■	■	⟋	⊙
310			•⟋	
317	↑	↑		
350	◡	◡		
351	★	★		
352	2	2		
353	H	H		
435	✳	✳		
436	‡			
445	▲	▲		
472	◇	◇		

•*2-ply*
Key continued on next page

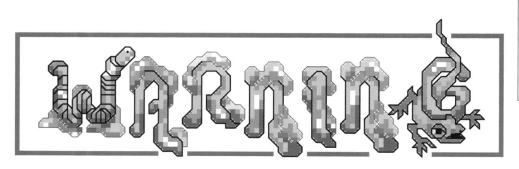

Key continued

DMC	X	1/4	BS	FK
666	♥	♥		
676	C	C		•
738	☆	☆		
747	Z	Z		
762	S	S		
801	✚	✚		
831	●	•		
833	▲	▲		
905	♣	♣	⬚	
906	⊥	⊥		
907	5	5		
922	✕	✕		
971	✿	✿		
3607	L	L		
3608	⅞	⅞		
3609	I	I		
3825	T	T		
3844	✗	✗	⬚	
3846	◼	◼		

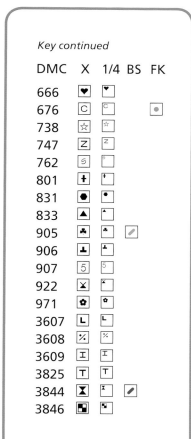

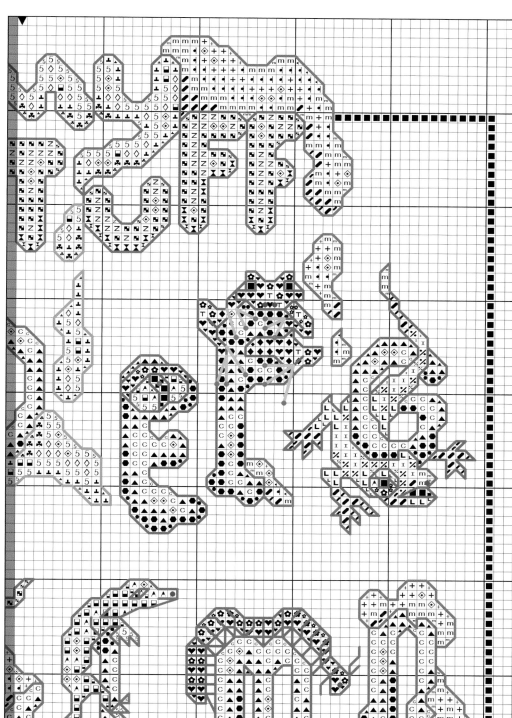

Top 2

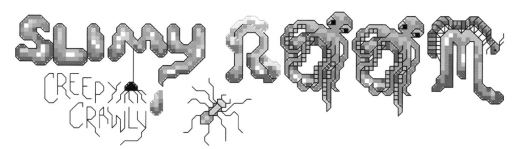

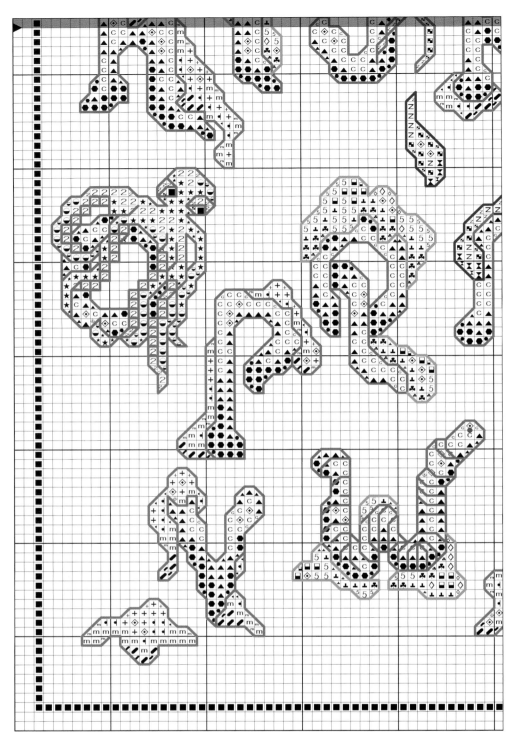

Bottom 1

Key continued

DMC	X	1/4	BS	FK
666	♥	♥		
676	C	C		●
738	☆	☆		
747	Z	Z		
762	5	5		
801	✚	✚		
831	⬢	●		
833	▲	▲		
905	♣	♣	╱	
906	⊥	⊥		
907	5	5		
922	✕	✕		
971	⬟	⬟		
3607	L	L		
3608	∕	∕		
3609	I	I		
3825	T	T		
3844	✖	✖	╱	
3846	◼	◼		

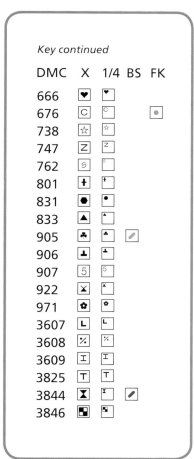

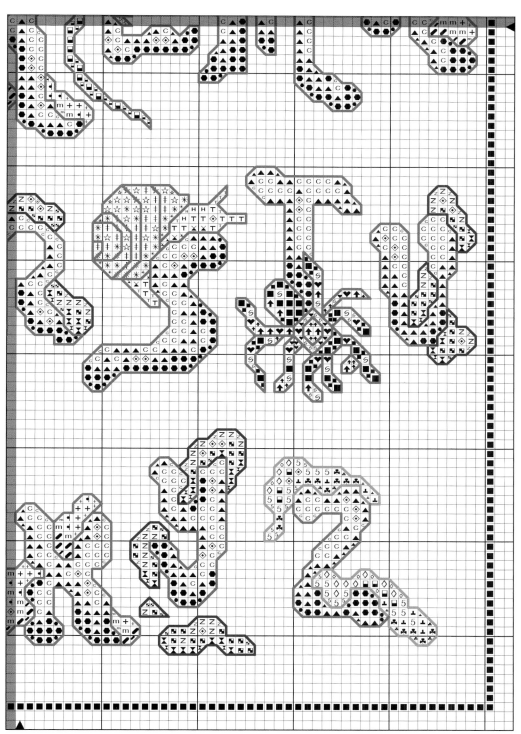

Bottom 2

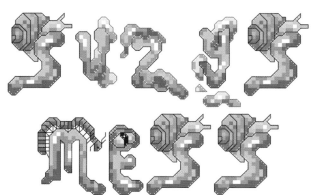

Section 1

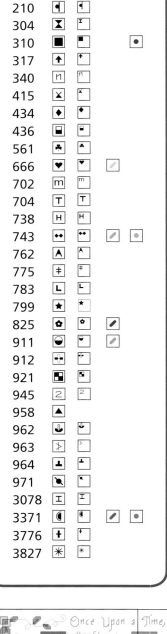

Once Upon a Time
Size: 168 x 84

DMC	X	1/4	BS	FK
1	◈	◈	✎	•
208	✖	✖		
210	◀	◀		
304	⊠	⊠		
310	■	■		•
317	↑	↑		
340	n	n		
415	✕	✕		
434	◆	◆		
436	▣	▣		
561	♣	♣		
666	♥	♥	✎	
702	m	m		
704	T	T		
738	H	H		
743	◆◆	◆◆	✎	•
762	A	A		
775	‡	‡		
783	L	L		
799	★	★		
825	✿	✿	✎	
911	◖	◖	✎	
912	◆◆	◆◆		
921	◼	◼		
945	2	2		
958	▲			
962	⚓			
963	▷	▷		
964	⊥	⊥		
971	◣	◣		
3078	I	I		
3371	◖	◖	✎	•
3776	✛	✛		
3827	✳	✳		

42

Time, there were

Section 2

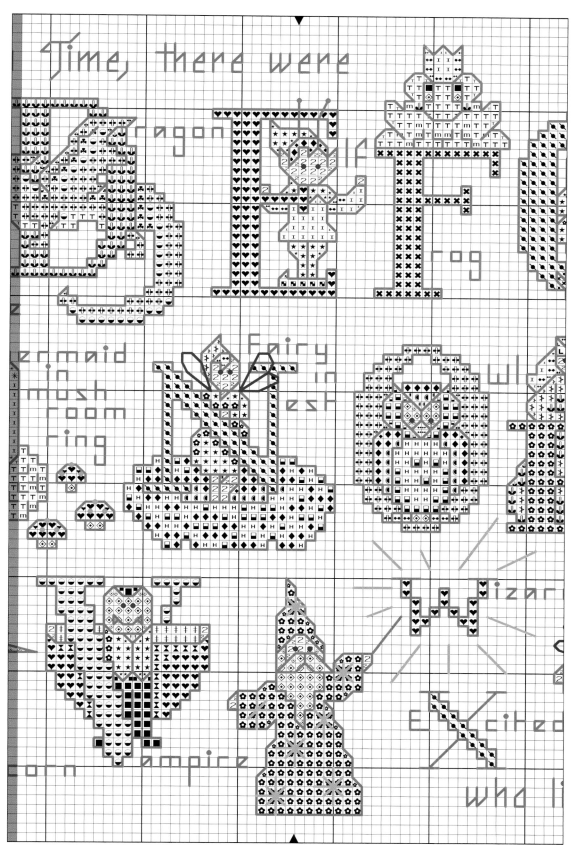

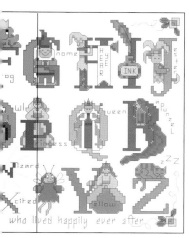

who lived happily ever after.

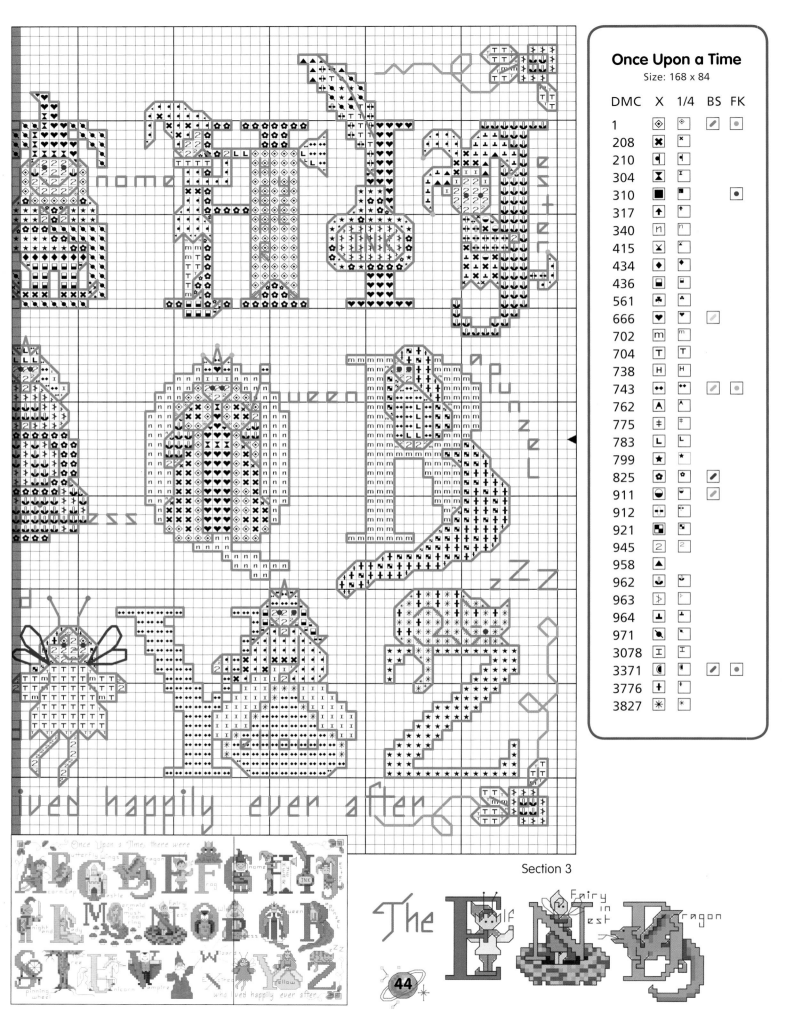

DMC	X	1/4	BS	FK
1	◈	◈	✎	•
208	✖	✖		
210	◀	◀		
304	✖	✖		
310	■	■		•
317	✦	✦		
340	n	n		
415	✕	✕		
434	◆	◆		
436	▣	▣		
561	♣	♣		
666	♥	♥	✎	
702	m	m		
704	T	T		
738	H	H		
743	✦✦	✦✦	✎	•
762	A	A		
775	‡	‡		
783	L	L		
799	★	★		
825	✿	✿	✎	
911	◖	◖	✎	
912	✦✦	✦✦		
921	◪	◪		
945	②	②		
958	▲			
962	⬇	⬇		
963	⟩	⟩		
964	⊥	⊥		
971	◣	◣		
3078	I	I	✎	•
3371	◖	◖	✎	•
3776	✚	✚		
3827	✳	✳		

Section 3